THE
ISAAC
FACTOR

Getting Ready For More of the Holy Spirit

BRUCE ATKINSON

RIVER

PUBLISHING

River Publishing & Media Ltd
info@river-publishing.co.uk

ISBN 978-1-908393-80-7
Cover design by www.spiffingcovers.com

Contents

DEDICATION

Dedicated to my son Jacob, a true Isaac.

καὶ ἐξῆλθεν Ισαακ ἀδολεσχῆσαι εἰς τὸ πεδίον τὸ πρὸς δείλης καὶ
ἀναβλέψας τοῖς ὀφθαλμοῖς εἶδεν καμήλους ἐρχομένας

Preface

I gave myself 7/10.

Emerging from one of those testing times we all experience during our journey to spiritual maturity, I thought I had acquitted myself well.

I'd taken the difficult situation I was in time and again to the Lord in prayer. I had also identified which fruit of the Holy Spirit I thought God was cultivating in me during this season, and did my best to cooperate with him.

Daily I trusted the Lord, asking him for help to quench any eruption of the fiery passions of the flesh that might impede my progress.

Yes a good, solid 7/10!

It was one of those trials I never want to go through again – *ever*. Yet, on reflection, I marvel at how the Holy Spirit forged character and purified faith in me through it. Later, as I was meditating on what had occurred I sensed the Holy Spirit speak to me, deep on the inside. He said words to this effect:

"Well done, you passed the test, but you still aren't ready for my greatest test…"

He had yet to finish his sentence, but already alarm bells rang loudly in my soul. Fear gripped me. "What will this greatest test be?" I asked myself. I feared for my family's health. Other disaster scenarios flashed through my mind. What could this great test be? The Lord continued to finish his sentence:

"Well done you passed the test, but you still aren't ready for my greatest test … the test of my blessing."

To be honest, until this moment I had never really thought of God's blessing as being a test. There was no course module in my theology degree entitled, *Preparing to Handle the Blessing 101*.

As I meditated on this word from the Holy Spirit I began to think about what kind of person I would need to become to handle the test of his blessing. Also, if I could figure out what was the greatest blessing God could give me, wouldn't that help me in preparing for it?

It occurred to me that the greatest blessing God can give any person is the Holy Spirit in great measure. The more the Holy Spirit's influence and power resides in our lives, surely the greater the blessing? Holy Spirit revivals are the greatest blessing God can bestow upon people on earth, because they are outpourings of heaven itself.

I felt certain that God had spoken clearly: the greatest test we can ever face is how we handle more of the Holy Spirit! To that end, what type of people do we need to become in order to successfully steward and secure the blessings of the Holy Spirit? What kind of person will pass "the test of this blessing?"

I remembered that Dr R.T. Kendall refers to the last great end-time outpouring of the Holy Spirit as "Isaac" and Paul identified genuine believers as "Isaacs" in his letter to the Galatians:

> "Now you, brothers, like Isaac, are children of promise."
> (Galatians 4:28)

Perhaps the sort of person who can handle more of the Holy Spirit's blessing will be like an Isaac?

Studying the character of Isaac, I became persuaded that he was indeed a role model for the Spirit-filled Christian. Isaac seems to me to be like an Old Testament personification of the fruit of the Holy Spirit. I have come to the conclusion that if anyone wants to handle the blessing of God in a serious way, they must become an "Isaac". Very few people seem aware of this vital factor, which is the reason for writing this book.

The Isaac Factor is a call for us to be ready for more of the Holy Spirit. We don't want to hinder him, or be ignorant of his workings. Rather, we want to become his competent partners in his gospel ministry. Sober and alert to the Spirit's activity, our hearts must become like soft clay in his hands, ready to be moulded; our minds attuned to his thoughts; our lives ready to be used and anointed with the Holy Ghost and with fire.

Let's get ready for more of the Holy Spirit!

Bruce Atkinson

It occurred to me that the greatest blessing that God could give to any one was the Holy Spirit and in great measure ... Revivals are the greatest blessing God can bestow upon people on earth because they are outpourings of heaven itself.

Chapter 1
Preparing for the Blessing of God

"For the LORD your God is bringing you into a good land, a land of brooks of water, of fountains and springs, flowing out in the valleys and hills, a land of wheat and barley, of vines and fig trees and pomegranates, a land of olive trees and honey, a land in which you will eat bread without scarcity, in which you will lack nothing, a land whose stones are iron, and out of whose hills you can dig copper. And you shall eat and be full, and you shall bless the LORD your God for the good land he has given you.

[Deuteronomy 8:7-10]

Are you ready to enter into God's blessing?

Of course I am!

Well, wait just a moment. Don't be too hasty with your answer. Even Moses had to give a final briefing to his people before they were ready to enter into the Promised Land. Moses spoke of the wonderful blessings ahead of them, but also warned that such blessings carried dangers with them too. Are you aware of the dangers of being blessed by God?

Read the whole of Deuteronomy chapter 8 right now, if you can.

Moses recounts the story of Israel's long journey with God. The wilderness years had been a time of great challenge, failure, humiliation and chastisement. As difficult a time as it was, however, through it all God had a plan to prepare his people for the blessing to come.

Moses reiterates how God had needed to teach them the lesson that "man does not live on bread alone" but by his promised word. Otherwise, in this new land where their bread (manna) and water diet would become a luxurious "milk and honey" feast, they might decide to toss his word aside as unimportant.

Moses didn't want them to forget that for forty years God miraculously kept their clothes from wearing out. True, they may have been 40 years out of fashion, but at least their clothes and shoes were kept in good working order! The Lord was teaching them to be thankful for his small mercies during the lean times, so that they would appreciate all the more the blessings of the good times to come.

This is a challenge for us. Do you keep your appreciation for all God has done for you, even during your lean times?

> *"In the wilderness He fed you manna which your fathers did not know, that He might humble you and that He might test you, to do good for you in the end."* (Deuteronomy 8:16 NASB)

The Apostle Paul realised that the experiences of Moses' generation with God were written down for the benefit of New Testament believers (1 Corinthians 10:6). Learning from the lives of others in the Bible, we can uncover the principles of how God prepares his people for great blessing – and then read about how they cope with that blessing when it arrives.

God is preparing you for something special. I wonder how you will handle it when it comes?

We've seen that the Promised Land was both a blessing and a danger at the same time. Would God's people be mature enough to steward well the blessing when it finally came? We need to understand that having God's blessing can spoil the immature, just as the immature can spoil God's blessing. If you really want to be blessed you must become spiritually mature – otherwise you are travelling on a road to ruin.

Remember the journey that got you here

Here is the danger of the Promised Land: as God's people enjoyed its many blessings, would they soon forget the lessons learnt from the journey they had travelled? Would they forget how God had saved them from slavery in Egypt? How he had delivered them from Pharaoh, sustained them, and guided them by his presence? Worse still, might they begin to believe that they deserved this blessing? That it was their right?

Here is one of the dangers of God's blessing: that having received it, you begin to get used to it and take it for granted. Eventually you may believe that in some way you are entitled to it – that you deserve it.

What would you do if you received everything you'd ever prayed for? Your dream job or that big promotion. The recognition you've always craved. The success you've desired, and the income to go with it. The ideal spouse. Imagine if God had simply ticked off your entire list of requests – would people still see you at worship on a Sunday? Would discipleship group meetings still be a priority in your diary? Would you still be a sacrificial follower of Jesus of Nazareth?

Do you understand what I'm getting at here?

That which we think of as a blessing can turn into a curse if we are not equipped to handle it. In Scripture, the Apostle James reserved the most stinging rebukes imaginable for rich people, because he knew that material blessings tend to cause people to stop trusting the Lord.

The poor Christian has no option but to trust the Lord. The rich believer may think they already have all the resources they need.

The greatest blessing of all

Proper stewarding of material wealth is important, but such blessings are secondary compared to God's greatest blessing. We cannot even begin to compare the temporal (earthly) blessings of God with his spiritual blessings. The greatest blessing he has made available to us on earth today is the gift of his Holy Spirit.

> *"What father among you, if his son asks for a fish, will instead of a fish give him a serpent; or if he asks for an egg, will give him a scorpion? If you then, who are evil, know how to give good gifts to your children, how much more will the heavenly Father give the Holy Spirit to those who ask him!"* (Luke 11:11-12)

In his gospel, Matthew explains that Jesus taught his disciples to expect "good things" from their Father in heaven. Luke describes how Jesus also taught that all these *good things* could be summed up in the giving of the Holy Spirit. When the Holy Spirit comes powerfully into a person's life, he brings along with him everything you could ever need.

The Holy Spirit is the chief executive of the Trinity, working on earth today. Jesus and the Father are in heaven, so it is the Holy Spirit who brings their heavenly power to those of us who follow Jesus.

The Bible is full of precious promises to help us in life, but all of God's promises put together can be found in experiencing the Father's promise of the Holy Spirit:

"And behold, I am sending the promise of my Father upon you. But stay in the city until you are clothed with power from on high." (Luke 24:49)

"And Peter said to them, 'Repent and be baptized every one of you in the name of Jesus Christ for the forgiveness of your sins, and you will receive the gift of the Holy Spirit. For the promise is for you and for your children and for all who are far off, everyone whom the Lord our God calls to himself.'" (Acts 2:38-39)

The real blessing of Abraham was never the Promised Land of Canaan, but rather the promised gift of the Holy Spirit

"So that in Christ Jesus the blessing of Abraham might come to the Gentiles, so that we might receive the promised Spirit through faith." (Galatians 3:14)

We aren't inheriting a Promised Land, we are inheriting the Promised Spirit!

Foretaste of Heaven

"And we believers also groan, even though we have the Holy Spirit within us as a foretaste of future glory, for we long for our bodies to be released from sin and suffering. We, too, wait with eager hope for the day when God will give us our full rights as his

adopted children, including the new bodies he has promised us." (Romans 8:23 NLT)

The samples of heaven that we see on earth are a foretaste of future glory that we can experience right now!

***

Have you ever been in a supermarket when they are running a special promotion? There are always samples. Perhaps a new brand of cheese, cut up and presented as little cubes on cocktail sticks?

"Would you care to sample the cheese sir?"

"Yes please," I reply, tasting a sample. "Mm, lovely."

I take another cube of cheese and the promoter's eyes narrow slightly.

"Yes, really nice!"

I reach out for some more.

"Sir," the person says, protecting the sample tray. "These are just samples. If you want more you can buy a full packet for £4 in aisle 6!"

Has anyone else been there, or is it just me?

The Holy Spirit brings "samples" of the kingdom of heaven into our broken, sinful world. He is our foretaste and guarantee of heaven (Romans 8:23; 2 Corinthians 5:5; Ephesians 1:13-14). He takes from heaven and brings to earth. He brings us to Jesus so that we can encounter him and he initiates heavenly activities within our earthly sphere of existence. As we pray for God's kingdom to come, and his will to be done on earth, as it is in heaven, it is the Holy Spirit who responds with action.

Full salvation will come to us only when the Lord returns, but until then, may we receive greater "samples" and foretastes of his kingdom power. Unlike the supermarket promoter, the Holy Spirit will allow us to partake of as much heavenly samples as we desire. Indeed, sometimes the Holy Spirit has been known to turn up in such power that it seems like believers nearly get the "whole cheese"!

God is preparing you for something special. I wonder how you will handle it when it comes? ... We need to understand that having God's blessing can spoil the immature, just as the immature can spoil God's blessing. If you really want to be blessed you must become spiritually mature – otherwise you are travelling on a road to ruin.

Chapter 2
This is That...

"But this is that which was spoken by the prophet Joel."

(Acts 2:16 KJV)

One night I couldn't sleep, so I reached for my headphones. I thought, "I'll listen to my audio Bible until I feel sleepy." What should I listen to? I thought perhaps Joel, as it's only three chapters long and I would probably feel drowsy by the end.

I've read Joel many times before, but I never sat and listened to the entire prophecy in one sitting. While listening, I remembered that on the Day of Pentecost (Acts 2) when the Holy Spirit was first poured out, the apostle Peter explained the occasion by recalling Joel's prophecy.

Hearing it as a whole helped me to understand the verses Peter chose to quote even more, given the context in which they were set.

In Joel's time God's people had grown careless in their attitude towards him. The Lord had no place whatsoever in their self-centred, self-indulgent lives. At best, God was found in the distant margins of community life. He found himself very low down, if not at the bottom, of people's daily to-do lists. They didn't really "do God" any more. If the Father had left the people to their own devices, they may well have remained "God-less" for the rest of their lives.

> "God whispers to us in our pleasures, speaks to us in our conscience, but shouts in our pains: it is his megaphone to rouse a deaf world." – C.S. Lewis

God cared for his people too much to leave them as they were. He yearned for a deeper fellowship with those who had forgotten him. In his mercy he sent a series of divine interruptions to get their attention. He sent successive locust plagues to destroy everything that distracted the people from him. Sometimes God's love can seem ruthless! But this is only because his loving desire towards us is so strong and passionate. True love can't tolerate any rivals and anything that competes with God in our lives is ultimately harmful to us.

Unfamiliar interruptions in your life's routine are usually signals from God that he is calling you to seek him in a new and profound way.

The locusts were God's way of sobering up his people from the inebriating effects of worldliness. The plagues served as loud foghorns, warning lives of impending spiritual shipwreck. The people may or may not have realised it at the time, but God was doing this for their own good. He was chastening them now, in order to bless them in the future.

Can you relate to this happening in your life?

Joel 2:13-14 cautions us,

> "Return to the LORD your God,
> for he is gracious and merciful,
> slow to anger, and abounding in steadfast love;
> and he relents over disaster.
> Who knows whether he will not turn and relent,
> and leave a blessing behind him."

Fortunately, the people came to their senses and returned to the Lord. He was back at the top of their "to do" list and now he was ready to send the blessing.

Today, you should know that God is calling you back to him in order to bless you!

William Butler Yeats wrote, "Tread softly because you tread on my dreams."

Have the "locusts of life" been gobbling up all your dreams? Have you experienced promises being broken, relationships that have failed? Have your hopes and expectations been replaced by feelings of hopelessness and despair? Perhaps you're caught in a trap and you can't walk out? Then the message of Joel is for you today!

By disturbing your routine, God is calling you to himself – all to prepare you for a wonderful, fresh outpouring of his Holy Spirit. Then new heavenly visons and dreams of life will come and they will not disappoint you.

A brand new season has arrived where the "that" which Joel spoke about will become a "this" in your experience:

> *"But **this is that** which was spoken by the prophet Joel; 'And it shall come to pass in the last days,' saith God, 'I will pour out of my Spirit upon all flesh: and your sons and your daughters shall prophesy, and your young men shall see visions, and your old men shall dream dreams. And on my servants and on my handmaidens I will pour out in those days of my Spirit; and they shall prophesy.'"* (Acts 2:16-18 KJV)

CHAPTER 3
THE ISAAC
FACTOR

"Now you, brothers, like Isaac, are children of promise."

(Galatians 4:28)

"What are you preaching on at the weekend Bruce?" asked a prominent pastor.

"I'm starting a new three-part series on Isaac," I replied.

"Isaac?! How can you find enough about him for a three-part series? He's one of the most boring, insipid, characters in the whole Bible. Give me Jacob over Isaac anytime. I could preach on him for months!"

This is a very common problem:

the overlooking of Isaac.

How many sermons have you heard on Isaac? How many books have been written about his life, compared to other biblical characters? His father, Abraham, was a spiritual giant, much referred to in both Old and New Testaments. But where would Abraham have been without Isaac? His whole life was defined in relation to the boy, because Isaac was the spiritual foundation for Abraham's entire relationship with God. The highs and lows of Abraham's friendship with God were in some way all connected to Isaac. From the low of the Ishmael concern, to the high of the "sacrifice" of Isaac, it is impossible to think of Abraham's relationship with God without Isaac somehow being right there in the middle of it.

Abraham the model of faith. Isaac the model of identity

Abraham provides a great model of faith for us to learn from. Examining his life, we see great instances of faith, but also incredible occasions of unbelief. Abraham's immaturity and struggles with unbelief eventually developed into an almost perfect trust in God. His historic footsteps of faith are definitely worth following:

> *"And he is then also the father of the circumcised who not only are circumcised but who also follow in the footsteps of the faith that our father Abraham had before he was circumcised."* (Romans 4:12 NIV)

Like our father Abraham, we who also believe are on a faith-maturing journey of working out our trust issues with the Lord.

I'm Isaac

I was brushing my teeth one morning, staring in the mirror and feeling really bad about myself. Have you ever had one of those moments? I was reflecting on what a rotten Christian I was! Would I ever become spiritually mature? It didn't seem like it at the time.

Just then, a phrase popped into my mind: *I'm Isaac.*

I shook my head and carried on brushing my molars. The phrase came again, but stronger this time. *I'm Isaac.*

"I'm not Isaac," I thought to myself. "I'm Ishmael, or at best Jacob."

The phrase repeated itself and I felt a growing urge to give voice to it. I looked in the mirror and whispered quietly to myself, "I'm Isaac." Tears appeared in my eyes. I said it again, then one more time, but now with a growing note of confidence. Deep in my heart I knew something spiritually powerful had just transpired.

Through this experience I discovered my spiritual identity. It would take me months to work out theologically the significance of that "toothbrush" encounter with the Holy Spirit, but my immediate response was to begin a serious study of the significance of Isaac in the Bible.

At the beginning of this chapter I quoted Galatians 4:28. Paul was reminding the legalistically-inclined Galatians of their true identity. Just like Isaac, they were children of the promise. Notice that Paul doesn't call them "Abrahams" because he was their spiritual father. Instead he calls them "Isaacs" because this is their identity and they need to discover it.

Why don't you say it for yourself, out loud, right now:

"I'm Isaac."

Say it again: "I'm Isaac."

One more time please and this time stronger: "I'm Isaac."

Yes, you really are!

Dr R.T. Kendall has a chapter entitled "Isaac" in his book *Holy Fire* (Charisma House, 2014). In it he describes a conference in London in 1992, during which he spoke of the current Pentecostal and Charismatic movements as an "Ishmael" in contrast to the next move of God to come, which he then characterised as "Isaac". I attended that conference and RT's emphasis on the coming Isaac move of God further spurred my interest in this patriarch.

If the next move of God is indeed to be regarded as *Isaac* and our *Isaac identity* is very much at the heart of Christian character for this season, then surely this must have tremendous ramifications for us. Perhaps there is a crucial *Isaac Factor* that will be pivotal in the transformation of an Ishmael generation into an Isaac generation? I believe there is.

Waiting for Isaac

We all know that it normally takes nine months from the point of conception until a baby is born. But when God told Abraham and Sarah that they would have a child, it took twenty-five years until Isaac was finally born.

Why did it take so long?

God was teaching Abraham and Sarah the spiritual discipline of *waiting*. For much of that twenty-five year period the aging couple couldn't understand why the promise was taking so long. Eventually, they lost patience with God and took matters into their own hands. Thus Ishmael was born to Abraham and Hagar.

They hadn't yet understood the truth that waiting for the promise of God is as important as eventually *receiving it.*

Instant coffee, instant Netflix series, instant food, instant social media and instant gratification… We have definitely lost the art of waiting. But we see that as important as the actual birth of Isaac was, the process of waiting was equally important because it fashioned and developed Abraham's character. Only when Abraham was spiritually ready would Isaac be born. Abraham had thought that he was ready years earlier, but God recognised that more time was needed before he was truly prepared to handle the Isaac blessing.

God commonly allows his children a period of waiting before giving them what he promises. All of us have a very strong tendency to overestimate ourselves. We think we are ready to handle the blessing of God now, when He knows that we aren't.

Joseph thought that he was ready to rule the moment he received his boyhood dreams, but we all know that it took years of subsequent preparation before his character was honed to be capable of being Pharaoh's right hand man.

If you are waiting for your *Isaac*, be encouraged. God is very much at work in your life. The Apostle James encourages us to let patience (or endurance) complete its full work in us, so that we become mature, complete and lacking nothing, ready to handle his blessing (James1:4). Don't fall into an Ishmael trap through impatience.

Persistent prayer brings the blessing

In Luke chapter 11 Jesus teaches his disciples the famous Lord's

Prayer. Immediately afterwards, he emphasises the need for persistence in prayer. We learn that our waiting for the promises of God should display itself most poignantly in prayer. Jesus encouraged the disciples to knock and keep knocking, to ask and keep asking, to seek and keep seeking until the door opened. Until the request was granted and that which was sought was found.

Jesus reminds us that our Father is more loving than any human parent and will give the Holy Spirt to those who continue to ask in prayer. There is a lesson here for us don't you think? I am convinced that genuine prayer is not just a means, but an end in itself, because through persistent, trusting prayer, God is preparing us; readying us for the time when the answer comes.

The joy of Isaac

Twenty-five years of waiting, enduring pain, fear and failure, ended with the birth of Isaac. The promise had finally arrived. The name Isaac literally means "laughter". Our journeys with God may take us through many dangers, toils and snares, but the destination is always a place of joy.

God does not keep his church in a permanent state of joyful revival for a number of reasons. One is that a period of waiting and longing for a fresh outpouring of the Holy Spirit is as spiritually important as when the next outpouring finally occurs.

God is as powerfully at work when he hides his face as when he manifests his presence publicly. He is as active behind the scenes as he is when he decides to take centre stage. It takes time for God's people to become ready for the next move of his Spirit, but for the patient not a moment is lost in waiting.

Learn that waiting on the Lord has a great and intentional purpose in your life. When the blessing comes you will be ready, prepared and oh-so grateful!

Isaac and Ishmael

"For it is written that Abraham had two sons, one by a slave woman and one by a free woman. But the son of the slave was born according to the flesh, while the son of the free woman was born through promise." (Galatians 4:22-23)

If we are children of the promise, just like Isaac, then surely we should become like him?

Notice that though Abraham petitioned God to accept Ishmael as the child of promise (Genesis 17:18), God refused. Isaac and Ishmael were polar opposites. In Galatians 4:21-31 Paul compares the two boys, then asks the Galatians to make sure that they identify themselves with Isaac, not Ishmael.

Ishmael was the product of human reasoning and effort. Isaac was the fulfilment of God's promise, brought about by a miraculous work of the Holy Spirit. Ishmael sprang from unbelief, but Isaac was birthed through faith. Ishmael signified bondage, but Isaac freedom. Ishmael resented Isaac and persecuted him because they were so different.

Paul pointed out to the Galatians that they were Isaacs, yet they were living like Ishmaels. That's where they had gone wrong.

The example of Isaac

Isaac was born by the will of Almighty God. We too were "born again" – not by human agency, but by supernatural power and resolve of God (John 1:12). Isaac was a miracle of God and so are we! You are a supernatural new creation of the living God!

So what is our "Isaac nature" like? What are the Isaac factors that cause us to stand apart from the crowd of Ishmaels in this world? I believe that Isaac is an Old Testament picture of the fruits of the Holy Spirit (Galatians 5:22-23). All the nine fruits of Spirit are found embedded in his life story.

In Genesis chapters 24-26 we find some key *Isaac factors*. Understanding and adopting these characteristics will be indispensable in helping us get ready for more of the Holy Spirit.

1. Take it to the Lord in prayer

"And Isaac went out to meditate in the field toward evening. And he lifted up his eyes and saw, and behold, there were camels coming." (Genesis 24:63)

If Isaac was anything he was a man of prayer.

This verse is a beautiful window into Isaacs's inner spiritual life. Born of a miracle, Isaac continued throughout his life to rely on the same supernatural power of God that birthed him. This power chiefly flowed into his life through the means of prayer.

On this occasion, whilst Isaac is praying the answer appears. A wonderful moment occurs as Isaac finishes praying, opens his eyes and there is the answer to his prayer standing right before him! Abraham had previously sent his own servant to find Isaac a wife, and the servant prayed and trusted the Lord to find the right one. Isaac was not sent, but he was supervising the whole situation through prayer.

Facetime with God

The word "meditate" can also be translated as "to pray", "to talk", "to chatter", "to think" and even "to complain". After the business of the day, Isaac sought refuge from the hustle and bustle of managing a huge tribe with all its servants and livestock. He did this by seeking solitude with God in the fields.

Alone with God was where the real business of his life was accomplished. Isaac sought the mind of the Spirit, knowing that success in the public place comes from the prayer in the secret place. He needed time each day to detox from a polluted world and charge his spiritual batteries. Isaac meditated on God's faithfulness in the past to help him trust the Lord in the present. Fears needed to be worked through, disappointments discussed, his will surrendered and the blessings of the following day secured.

That's what he was doing in his field. Where's your field?

Imagine Isaac's joyful surprise when his most important prayer request literally appeared before his eyes. As Isaac says his final "Amen", he opens his eyes and there she is: his Rebekah!

You will find that during persistent prayer there can be long periods of silence from God. But then out of the blue the answer comes, both suddenly and unexpectedly. God likes to surprise people. Even on the Day of Pentecost, after seeking the Spirit for fifty days in an upper room, as the followers of Jesus continued to dwindle, the Holy Spirit finally came *suddenly*, like a violent rushing wind (Acts 2:2).

The first time Rebekah observed her future husband he was at prayer. It should be a single woman's greatest desire to wed a man of prayer and vice versa. Isaac is the only Old Testament patriarch who remained married to one woman. Rebekah was enough for him, even though in the culture of the day he could have also married other women or taken concubines. Isaac didn't follow the pervasive culture of the day to satisfy his carnal lusts. The man had the fruit of love and self-control.

Isaac wasn't perfect, of course, and he repeated his father mistakes. He pretended that his wife was his sister to save himself. Out of fear he told Abimelech and the men of Gerar that Rebekah was not his wife, because he hadn't matured in faith enough to trust God to guard him in the matter. It was then embarrassing when Abimelech caught him caressing her. But God's grace covered his immaturity (and thank God it also covers ours!)

> "And Isaac prayed to the LORD for his wife, because she was barren. And the LORD granted his prayer, and Rebekah his wife conceived." (Genesis 25:21)

When reading Genesis 25, don't blink or you may miss this verse. Just like his parents, Isaac and Rebekah were also barren – unable to conceive. But this time no servant girl was impregnated to solve the problem and Isaac didn't take another wife. The conception eventually took place through the means of prayer, which preceded the pregnancy in the natural. Isaac had the *fruit of patience and faith.*

Is there something that you are trying to "conceive" without prayer? Be careful because you might unleash an Ishmael into your life. Remember that believing, trusting prayer prepares us for the blessing of God whilst also bringing it to us. When the blessing is birthed, it continues to be nurtured and protected by the same prayerful attitude.

2. Isaac in famine

"And Isaac sowed in that land and reaped in the same year a hundredfold. The LORD blessed him, and the man became rich, and gained more and more until he became very wealthy. He had possessions of flocks and herds and many servants, so that the Philistines envied him." (Genesis 26:12-14)

Isaac's story shows that God's blessing is not dependent on your present environment. In fact, sometimes God will allow the environment you are in to be entirely in opposition to the blessing he has promised you. That way, when the blessing comes, God is glorified and we are all the more thankful. If Isaac had been blessed during a time of great plenty, would God's blessing in his life been evident as a work of the Holy Spirit?

Underwhelmed by the blessing?

The beginning of Genesis 26 tells us that there was a famine in the land, similar to the one faced by Abraham years earlier. After many years of journeying, Abraham finally arrived at his promised destination and instead of finding the red carpet waiting to welcome him, he found everyone checking out of Canaan just as he was checking in! The population was fleeing to Egypt where there was food. He had reached the Promised Land, but all he found was famine. How do you think he felt? How would you feel?

Sometimes we arrive at the place of blessing and find ourselves initially disappointed. "Oh, so this is it then?" If the blessing isn't what we'd envisaged or expected, we are somewhat disillusioned. Abraham was distinctly underwhelmed with what he found in Canaan, so before long he was leaving with everyone else. The environment was too uncomfortable to remain in. He journeyed away from the disappointing place God had sent him to and travelled to Egypt. It was there that all his troubles began.

God's blessing can appear in inauspicious places and be hard to discern. Mankind's greatest ever blessing appeared in apparent poverty in the stable of a small inn. The rain that ended a drought began as an insignificant cloud no bigger than a man's hand (1 Kings 18:44). Jesus likened the kingdom of God to a tiny mustard seed and invisible yeast. The Bible teaches us not to despise the day of small things (Zechariah 4:10). We must learn to appreciate the small, kingdom seeds we receive, or we might miss out when one day they become mighty oaks.

God didn't want Isaac to make the same mistake as Abraham. He told him not to go down to Egypt. We can learn from Isaac that we should stay wherever God has planted us, even if our environment seems very uncomfortable. Better to be an Isaac and stay in God's difficult place of promise than to run away. The grass may look greener in "Egypt" but it is most certainly not. Abraham learnt that painful lesson. If God has planted you in difficult circumstances, don't run away. Those circumstances will pass, but you will remain – but now with a greater blessing than before.

Overwhelmed by the blessing!

Isaac sowed in famine. What a lesson for us in times of lack. In a time of "no blessing" Isaac sowed for a great blessing. He didn't eat his last seed, he planted it. Sometimes it may seem to us that the Holy Spirit has withdrawn his blessing. It may appear like this for a season, but this doesn't mean the Lord has stopped working amongst us. It just means he has taken his work underground for a while. He will resurface!

As in the natural, so in the spiritual. It can't be harvest season all the time. Sometimes in life we need to go through an arid winter. Our spiritual strength seems to recede from public view, but in fact the Holy Spirit is working deep in our spiritual root system. The winter season might be hard going, but this preparation will make us hardy and robust, ready for the arrival of a new spring season of promise. We need the autumn and winter seasons of life, as well as the spring and summer, to become fully mature and fruitful. What season are you in right now?

Isaac continued to believe God through a famine situation, where everything looked bleak. He trusted in the promises of God, despite his deteriorating circumstances. He believed that the Lord was still busy behind the scenes. During this period of Isaacs's life a great work took place in him. His faith was purified by this harsh, unforgiving season, and it prepared him to enter a place of great blessing. The deep, hidden work of the Spirit that takes place in "famine" is just as important as the joy and outward blessing that comes during "harvest".

Because Isaac's sowing was supernatural, so too was his reaping! He became so enriched by God that his Philistine neighbours began to envy him. The blessing just kept flooding in.

3. The test of my blessing

"And Abimelech said to Isaac, 'Go away from us, for you are much mightier than we.'" (Genesis 26:16)

Isaac was blessed beyond belief – and because the blessing came so plentifully in the midst of a famine, it was emphasised all the more. How Isaac handled this incredible blessing of God is breath-taking to behold.

Isaac had become the "main man" – the most powerful person in the land. Other powerful people, like Abimelech, were so intimidated by him that they asked him to leave.

What would we do if we found ourselves in a similar position? We've been blessed with incredible wealth, power and influence where we have settled, and someone wants us to leave. It would be very tempting to respond, "That's right, I'm more powerful than you. You'll be the one leaving, not me!"

Isaac, however, wasn't corrupted or spoilt by God's blessing. The previous seasons he'd endured had prepared him. He knew that he was but a humble steward of all God's blessings. The power and wealth didn't go to his head. He refused to assert his power to crush another, even though he was capable. Instead, he sought to pursue peace from his position of power.

Again we see Isaac displaying what the New Testament would call the "fruit of the Holy Spirit". In this respect, he is in a different league to most of the characters in the Old Testament. He had no need to leave the place where he was established, but as a man of peace he moved on. Why?

Isaac recognised that God was the source of his blessing. No person or circumstance could interfere with that. To that end, it didn't matter where he was. He had been liberated from the need to grasp, grab and fight for earthly wealth, position and power. He was a free man, dependent on God and God alone. I am convinced that it was his powerful personal devotional life, taking place behind the scenes, that gave him such high levels of faith in the Lord.

The blessing of God will test you! Be warned, if you are unprepared for it, God's blessing may bring out the worst in you! This is why, in the midst of great revivals, there is often much rivalry, greed and jealousy. It is a consequence of immature, carnal people who are unable to cope with the powerful moving of the Holy Ghost.

Well, well, well...

So Isaac, the man of peace, took his leave. He gathered together his family, servants and livestock and left a green and pleasant land for a desert with no water. He suddenly found himself in the midst of a resource crisis. It seemed as though the way of peace had led to loss and danger. He must have felt a tremendous responsibility to provide for the hundreds of people and animals under his care.

At first glance, some might think Isaac was a weak man, but they would be wrong. He was the wealthiest businessman in the region, with extensive management responsibilities, stewarding many people and animals. As a result he carried a huge leadership burden in complex circumstances. If he'd been a weak man he wouldn't have been able to cope with any of this. In fact, Isaac ran such a smooth operation that the Bible has nothing to report to us about it. So how did he tackle his current dilemma?

Isaac set his men to work finding and re-digging wells to ensure that his family and herds would not perish. The first well they dug was challenged; local herdsman suddenly appeared claiming it for themselves. They hadn't so much as lifted a spade, but they still demanded it. Isaac could have swatted them away like flies, especially as the pressure for water was mounting. These men had no claim to a well they had neither discovered nor dug out. Isaac could have justifiably fought for and secured that well. But again, he rose above his circumstances, demonstrating a higher level of righteousness. Isaac gave them the well, naming it *Esek* (contention).

We might well applaud Isaac's act of magnanimity. But would we congratulate him for giving away the second well he finds? His find is challenged and once again he chooses not to contest it, this time naming it *Sitnah* after his "enemies".

How many of us would have let go of the first well we had toiled over, desperate for water, let alone a second? Was Isaac a weak man, fearful of confrontation? So timid and feeble that he allowed people to walk all over him?

No, Isaac fought his battles in the secret place, so that he didn't have to engage in bare knuckle fights in public. Rather, he felt empowered not only to tolerate his enemies, but even to bless them.

The third well, that none of us would have discovered because we'd still be fighting over the first two, was uncontested. Isaac named it *Rehoboth* meaning "broad places".

> *"And he moved from there and dug another well, and they did not quarrel over it. So he called its name Rehoboth, saying, 'For now the Lord has made room for us, and we shall be fruitful in the land.'"* (Genesis 26:22)

The point here is that *the Lord made room for Isaac*; he didn't forcefully make room for himself. If he had retaliated, fought and subjected his enemies, it would have stirred up resentment and hate. As it was, they must have been grudgingly impressed by the kind, patient way in which he dealt with them. God too was impressed with Isaac's actions over the wells. So much that the night after he found the third well, the Lord appeared to Isaac and blessed him even more mightily than before (Genesis 26:23-25). Isaac had proven that there wasn't a blessing from God he couldn't handle.

The binding

The binding of Isaac to be sacrificed by his father Abraham – the *Akedah*, as it is known in the Hebrew language – shows us both the culmination of Abraham's faith and the quintessence of Isaac's character.

Abraham had become such good friends with the Lord that he no longer had any trust issues in regard to God's character or his promises. When God commanded Abraham to sacrifice Isaac, he reasoned that because God had promised Isaac would produce his grandchildren in the future, if he were to sacrificially die then God would just have to raise him from the dead in order to fulfil his promise (Hebrews 11:17-19).

It also seems that Isaac wasn't a small child when Abraham took him to be sacrificed. Thus, he would have been able to resist if he so desired. There is a strong Rabbinic tradition that during the Akedah Isaac was a strong, healthy young man, well able to resist his father if he wanted to. But like Jesus, Isaac willingly obeyed his father's will for him to be sacrificed. In the end, a ram was provided by the Lord for the sacrifice, but Isaac's willingness had transformed him into a living sacrifice. Isaac is the finest Old Testament picture of Christ dying on the cross. Similarly, his passive submission to his father was his greatest act of faith.

Are you getting this? Are you seeing the incredible levels of godliness and faith Isaac had? How would you apply the lessons of Isaac to your situation right now?

This is your new identity in Christ. You are an Isaac. When we study the Sermon on the Mount later in this book, we will find that the principles of Spirit-filled living offer a stunning reflection of Isaac's character.

Unfamiliar interruptions in your
life's routine are usually signals from
God that he is calling you to seek
him in a new and profound way ...
By disturbing your routine, God is
calling you to himself – all to prepare
you for a wonderful, fresh outpouring
of his Holy Spirit.

Chapter 4
Ich Habe
Genug!

"'Lord,' he said, 'now I can die content! For I have seen him as you promised me I would. I have seen the Saviour you have given to the world.'"

(Luke 2:29 TLB)

Alone, driving in my car, it seemed like everything I had been working towards all my life had just suddenly vanished, like a puff of smoke. I turned on Radio 4 and an episode from their Soul Music series had just started. The programme was about a piece of music by J.S. Bach, a cantata called *Ich Habe Genug* in German, which translated means, "I have enough" or "I am content."

The cantata tells the story of Simeon, who was promised by the Holy Spirit that he would not die until he had seen the Messiah.

The radio programme had a number of different people talking about how this cantata had touched their lives during very trying personal circumstances. In the song, Simeon sings these words as he cradles the Christ-child in his arms:

It is enough
I have held the Saviour, the hope of all peoples,
In the warm embrace of my arms
It is enough

There is also a verse in the cantata imagining how Christians throughout history might have responded, had they been present at this poignant scene:

I have enough
My comfort is this alone
That Jesus might be mine and I his own
In faith I hold him
There I see, along with Simeon
Already the joy of the other life
Let us go with this man

The music is very beautiful and knowing the meaning of the words makes it hard to listen to without shedding a tear. I was deeply moved by both the programme and the music. I began to contemplate what it must have felt like for Simeon to literally hold the infant Jesus in his arms. The elation, the joy, the sense of fulfilment he must have experienced in that moment! All that he had ever lived for, hoped for and prayed for, he now held in his arms. Simeon no longer had any need to look to the future – he was totally absorbed in the moment of fulfilment. He was now ready for heaven. Jesus was enough. Nothing more was needed.

With my ordered life-plans in tatters, I needed to find myself where Simeon found himself that day, in the Temple. I felt a mounting desire to experience more and more of the Lord Jesus, so that one day soon I could sincerely declare "Ich habe genug."

In these days the Holy Spirit is guiding us all to a place where our hearts will sing, "Jesus is enough. I am content."

God commonly allows his children a period of waiting before giving them what he promises. All of us have a very strong tendency to overestimate ourselves. We think we are ready to handle the blessing of God now, when He knows that we aren't ... If you are waiting for your Isaac, be encouraged. God is very much at work in your life.

CHAPTER 5
THE JACOB
MALAISE

"Jacob answered Pharaoh, 'I have travelled on this earth for 130 years. The years of my life have been few and full of sorrow, and less than the years that my fathers lived.'"

(Genesis 47:9 NLV)

I fear that most of us haven't even begun the process of discovering the Isaac identity that has been placed within us. That doesn't mean that we are "Ishmaels" – every believer is a child of the promise, whether they act like it or not. But we have an identity crisis. I believe that the vast majority of us presently identify more with Jacob than Isaac. In fact, I suggest that identification with Jacob is so widespread in western Christian culture that I've given it a term:

The Jacob Malaise.

Malaise

The English Oxford Living dictionary defines malaise as, "A general feeling of discomfort, illness, or unease whose exact cause is difficult to identify." Examples of its usage are, "a general air of malaise" and "a society afflicted by a deep cultural malaise".

When Jacob met Pharaoh near the sunset of his life, he felt the need to apologise for his haggard appearance. He reflected that his life had been short; a hint of jealousy emerged in respect to the fact that his ancestors had lived longer and more blessed lives than he.

Jacob summarised his life by saying it was characterised by sorrow. Other Bible translations of Genesis 47:9 use words like unpleasant, difficult, evil and hard to describe his life. The reason why Jacob was such a wreck of a man at the end of his sorrow-filled life was because he had more faith in himself than he did in God. He didn't take his struggles to the Lord and ask for help – he tried to solve them himself. Jacob's impatience with God for not giving him what he thought he needed, and his need to control the people and events around him, were the prime causes of his misery.

Scripture shows us that God was always *for* Jacob, but not always *with* him – especially concerning the strategies he employed to pursue God's promised blessings. In this sense, I consider Jacob a great warning to us all; particularly those who serve in Christian leadership. We need to heed Jacob's mistakes as well as emulate Isaac's example.

The Jacob Malaise brings discontentment, discomfort, disharmony, disunity and disease into the body of Christ.

If Isaac grew in grace to fulfil his name – *laughter* – Jacob's egocentricity ensured that he lived up to his name – *struggler*.

Though Jacob was the spiritual heir to the promised blessing of God, just like Abraham and Isaac, he wrestled and grasped for his blessing. He wrestled with his twin brother in Rebekah's womb. The Lord's promise was that the older brother would be the servant of the younger, but as Easu came out of the womb first, Jacob grasped his leg and tried to pull him back in! This is a microcosm of Jacob's entire life; his *modus operandi* was to grab and grasp at the promises of God – but this is not how faith works.

Like his grandfather and father before him, the call on Jacob's life was to pursue God's promise by faith and patience. Jacob, however, didn't walk in his forefather's footsteps. If he had, his life story would read very differently.

Pursuing the promise by means of the flesh

Is it possible to pursue God's promises with selfish motives and carnal strategies? Absolutely. Is it even possible to attain some of those promises through self-centred living and man-made schemes? It certainly is. Jacob's life is testament to this. He managed to reach his spiritual "destination", but not by routes approved by God. As a result, he suffered greatly and ended his life in misery, a wreck of a man.

The end never justifies the means

The axiom often attributed to Machiavelli, "The end justifies the means" is not a Christian principle. "The means" are important to the Lord. *How* you achieve success in life, and the *way* in which you treat others in its pursuit are vital. We need to understand that "the end" is always in the Lord's hands. Isaac got this. Jacob didn't.

God had promised that one day Esau's birth right would belong to Jacob, but instead of waiting patiently for the promise, Jacob coldly, calculatingly took advantage of his brother when he was in a weak position (Genesis 25:29-34). We read that Esau arrived home exhausted and starving. Jacob had some bread and stew prepared, but used it to bribe his brother, withholding nourishment until his brother relinquished his birth right.

It's true that Esau despised his birth right, but Jacob acted in a nasty, manipulative way. What God has promised was effectively fulfilled, but do you think he was pleased that Jacob intervened and exploited someone's weakness? Did God want Jacob to take matters into his own hands, rather than trusting him, seeking his guidance to see the promise fulfilled? Of course not.

Jacob took by force what God had promised to give by grace. We must not do the same!

God had promised Jacob he would receive Isaac's blessing. Jacob believed the promise, but decided to take matters into his own hands – even stooping so low as to deceive his own father. Taking advantage of Isaac's old age he disguised himself as Esau in order to get the blessing by subterfuge (Genesis 17). When Isaac realised he had been tricked, he was so appalled and distressed that his body shook violently. Jacob extorted his blessing at the expense of his father's health. And how did Esau feel about it? Jacob's actions incited his brother to hatred – so much so that he plotted Jacob's murder.

Jacob's actions set in motion a series of consequences that would batter and bruise him for years. He found himself fleeing his home and, ironically, dealing with a man called Laban who was twice as manipulative as he was! When we sow in the flesh, rather than trusting the work of the Spirit, we can reap terrible consequences.

Later in life, when Jacob wrestled with God he got a blessing, but at the price of a disabled hip. Jacob walked with a limp for the rest of his life. Many Bible teachers use this episode as an illustration of how we must wrestle in prayer until we receive what we are asking for. I accept that, but my question is this: why didn't Jacob just submit to the angel like Isaac submitted to being bound? I think Jacob would still have been blessed.

As a father, Jacob's pattern of life continued. He spoiled his favourite son, Joseph, so much that it made his brother's jealous and stirred up resentment and murderous thoughts. Eventually they kidnapped him and sold him as a slave. Jacob suffered the consequences, spending years grieving for the son he thought dead, who was actually alive.

Don't be a Jacob, be an Isaac!

Having served in ministry for 30 years, I've seen quite a few Christians suffering from *The Jacob Malaise*. I suffer from occasional bouts of the malaise too. I'm asking the Holy Sprit to heal me and help the healthy Isaac within to arise. Let's embrace the Isaac factor and leave the Jacob malaise far behind, so we can handle more of God's promise of the Holy Spirit.

God is as powerfully at work when he hides his face as when he manifests his presence publicly. He is as active behind the scenes as he is when he decides to take centre stage. It takes time for God's people to become ready for the next move of his Spirit, but for the patient not a moment is lost in waiting.

CHAPTER 6
SMOKE AND FIRE

"A bruised reed he will not break, and a smouldering wick he will not quench, until he brings justice to victory."

(Matthew 12:20)

In his book *The Bruised Reed*, author Richard Sibbes writes,

"In pursuing his calling, Christ will not quench the smoking flax, or wick, but will blow it up till it flames. In smoking flax there is but a little light, and that weak, as being unable to flame, and that little mixed with smoke. The observations from this are that, in God's children, especially in their first conversion, there is but a little measure of grace, and that little mixed with much corruption, which, as smoke, is offensive; but that Christ will not quench this smoking flax."

The Bruised Reed is my favourite Christian book. First published in 1630 it still encourages struggling believers today. Perhaps at this moment you feel like a smouldering wick or a bruised reed – fragile and vulnerable? Are you worried that God will pour out his blessing on everyone else but you? When people talk of spiritual revival, are you just hoping for spiritual *survival*?

You'll burn on, not burn out

Sometimes our Christian lives seem more smoke than fire. Tough situations bruise us and we are hurt. People are unkind to us, dampening the burning Spirit in our hearts. Sometimes our lives seem to be full of toxic smoke rather than ablaze with the Holy Ghost's fire.

I have good news for you: no matter how bruised you are, Jesus won't allow you to break. However smoky are the burning embers of your faith, Christ will never allow your spark to be extinguished.

Have you ever tended a camp fire? You light it with dry kindling, let the fire build up, then place logs on for fuel. It burns bright, but left unattended the fire eventually abates. Perhaps when you return to the fire it looks like it has died – a pile of cold black soot. But camp fire experts know that under the soot, if you can find even a wisp of smoke, if you blow and keep blowing hard, soon what seemed dead will burn bright again.

The New Testament word for Spirit is *pneuma* in the Greek language. It can be translated *wind* as easily as *Spirit*. Jesus explained that the wind (or Spirit) blows wherever it wills (John 3:8). When the Holy Spirit entered the Upper Room on the day of Pentecost, he came with the sound of a rushing, mighty wind as tongues of fire appeared on the people there (Acts 2:2-3).

Notice the wind and fire of the Spirit! The Spirit's flame burned on the pure "wicks" of sanctified human hearts – those who had been seeking, cleansing and preparing themselves for the coming of the Spirit for the previous fifty days.

I recently bought one of those garden chimineas, so my family could sit outside even in the cool of the evening. The trouble was, the wood gave off so much smoke that our clothes would stink for days afterwards. Then I discovered smokeless fuel. Now there is no smoke, just heat and light!

May I encourage you to call on the Holy Spirit today? Even if feels like you have no fire left inside your heart. Surrender the smoking wick of your life to him afresh. Jesus is tending the fire in your heart and he won't let it be extinguished. His plan is for the Holy Spirit to blow a fresh wind over the cinders of your heart. You may not see the results immediately, but be patient. You will soon feel the effects of the Spirit's breath kindling tiny sparks into flames that will soon become a roaring fire. Don't worry about the excess "smoke" you are giving off at the moment. As the fire within develops, impurities are being burnt off by the Spirit. I prophesy that soon you will burn without smoke – pure and holy, radiating only light and heat!

Sometimes our Christian lives seem more smoke than fire. Tough situations bruise us and we are hurt. People are unkind to us, dampening the burning Spirit in our hearts ... I have good news for you: no matter how bruised you are, Jesus won't allow you to break ... Christ will never allow your spark to be extinguished.

Chapter 7
An Audience
of One

"And your Father who sees in secret will reward you." (Matthew 6:4)

Dr R.T. Kendall, in his book *The Sermon on the Mount* (Chosen Books) writes,

"The purpose of the Sermon on the Mount is to demonstrate the kind of teaching – and the kind of living with regard to character and conduct – that should govern the people of God through the power of the Holy Spirit."

The Sermon on the Mount is a blueprint for Spirit-filled Living...

If you begin to earnestly apply the teaching of Jesus' sermon to your daily life, with the Spirit's help you will soon look on the outside very much like the Isaac you are on the inside. Without the Spirit's help, however, it is impossible to put the principles into practice. For this Sermon to work through our daily lives we need a daily filling of the Holy Spirit; his leading and direction, backed up with a strong believing, trusting prayer life.

I've already said that in regard to character, Isaac is a picture of the fruit of the Spirit. So the Sermon on the Mount gives us a vital blueprint for living. Rather than present a commentary on the sermon (Matthew 5-7), however, I'd like to highlight a few of the crucial spiritual principles found within it. As we allow the Holy Spirit the freedom to work in our hearts, this sermon will gradually become our pattern for living.

The Holy Spirit works to the blueprint of the Sermon on the Mount

How is the Holy Spirit working in your life today? Whatever issue seems paramount at present, I can assure you he will be working in harmony with the principles of the Sermon on the Mount. Therefore, a good understanding of the sermon will help you to partner more effectively with what the Spirit is working to achieve in your life and through your circumstances.

The Be Attitudes

Jesus begins his sermon with eight Beatitudes. They have been nicknamed the Be Attitudes because they describe *the people we are becoming*, rather than *things we should be doing*. Christianity is a process of self-discovery. The attitudes described already reside within your born again nature. Surrendering to the Holy Spirit will cause the "new you" to begin to emerge and bear fruit. When you cooperate with the Spirit you increasingly become who you are!

Below is a contemporary translation of the Beatitudes for you to mediate on. They paint a striking portrait of the Spirit-filled person, describing the kind of fruitful attitudes that the Holy Spirit is cultivating in your heart. Notice how each Be Attitude attracts God's blessing. If you want to prepare to receive more of the blessing of God in your life, this is the type of person you need to become:

"When Jesus saw his ministry drawing huge crowds, he climbed a hillside. Those who were apprenticed to him, the committed, climbed with him. Arriving at a quiet place, he sat down and taught his climbing companions. This is what he said:

'You're blessed when you're at the end of your rope. With less of you there is more of God and his rule.

You're blessed when you feel you've lost what is most dear to you. Only then can you be embraced by the One most dear to you.

You're blessed when you're content with just who you are—no more, no less. That's the moment you find yourselves proud owners of everything that can't be bought.

You're blessed when you've worked up a good appetite for God. He's food and drink in the best meal you'll ever eat.

You're blessed when you care. At the moment of being "care-full", you find yourselves cared for.

You're blessed when you get your inside world—your mind and heart—put right. Then you can see God in the outside world.

You're blessed when you can show people how to cooperate instead of compete or fight. That's when you discover who you really are, and your place in God's family.

You're blessed when your commitment to God provokes persecution. The persecution drives you even deeper into God's kingdom.

Not only that—count yourselves blessed every time people put you down or throw you out or speak lies about you to discredit me. What it means is that the truth is too close for comfort and they are uncomfortable. You can be glad when that happens— give a cheer, even!—for though they don't like it, I do! And all heaven applauds. And know that you are in good company. My prophets and witnesses have always gotten into this kind of trouble.'" – The Message

The Holy Spirit works from the inside out

Oswald J. Smith said, "The heart of the human problem is the problem of the human heart." This is why God works in us from the inside out. He has to deal with our heart, not our superficial exterior.

The Pharisees never understood this principle. Their focus was on the external; concerned with the appearance of doing what was right. This is why Jesus called them out. Though a person may not have committed the physical act of murder, the anger in their heart declares them guilty (Matthew 5:21-22). Though a person may not have committed adultery, the lust raging in their heart and mind discredits them before God (Matthew 5:27-28). Every evil act begins in the heart:

"Do you not see that whatever goes into the mouth passes into the stomach and is expelled? But what comes out of the mouth proceeds from the heart, and this defiles a person. For out of the heart come evil thoughts, murder, adultery, sexual immorality, theft, false witness, slander." (Matthew 15:17-19)

Cleansed at the source

I heard a story about an isolated village situated at the foot of a large mountain. A terrible sickness spread rapidly amongst the people in the valley and everyone was becoming ill. Some were even dying. An emergency medical team flew into the valley in order to treat the people, but despite bringing different types of medicine, the community's health deteriorated. It seemed that no treatment would work.

One afternoon a doctor took a break from tending to the sick and wandered up the mountain. As she ascended higher, the doctor followed the course of the mountain stream that brought the water supply into the village. Eventually, high up the mountain, she discovered a deep pool – the source of the stream. In it was floating the bloated carcass of a mountain goat. It had somehow fallen into the pool and drowned. This was the cause of the sickness down in the village. They were all drinking water from a polluted source. It didn't matter what type of medicine was given to the villagers, they wouldn't get better until the source of their water was purified. Once the dead goat was removed, the villagers began to recover.

Our hearts are the source of everything that flows out of our lives – good or bad. A bad heart produces evil; a good heart, righteousness. This means that you cannot achieve lasting change simply by altering your outward actions – that's religion. True change takes place on the inside, where the Holy Spirit is at work. He is healing our hearts so that his living waters can flow out through our words and deeds.

> *"Whoever believes in me, as the Scripture has said, 'Out of his heart will flow rivers of living water.' Now this he said about the Spirit, whom those who believed in him were to receive, for as yet the Spirit had not been given, because Jesus was not yet glorified."* (John 7:38-39)

What's going on in your heart?

How is the Holy Spirit working in your heart right now? What is he placing his finger on today – what attitude that needs to be addressed? Remember, God never deals with everything that needs healing in our hearts all in one go – that would be too overwhelming for anyone. He graciously deals with one issue after another. An indication of what the Holy Spirit is presently doing in your heart can be found in your circumstances right now.

Are you facing a frustrating situation at the moment? Then you can be sure that God is working in you to produce faith and patience.

Does everything seem to be going wrong? Then your trust issues with God's faithfulness are being addressed.

If someone is treating you badly, the Lord is teaching you love and mercy, to be backed up with increased prayer.

If you are prospering and being successful, he is looking to work humility in you and produce a generosity towards others. He has blessed you to become a blessing.

Whatever godly attitudes or actions your current life circumstances are demanding, these are the clues to discover how the Holy Spirit is endeavouring to work maturity in you.

An audience of one

"All the world's a stage,
And all the men and women merely players;
They have their exits and their entrances."
– William Shakespeare (*As You Like It*)

In the real life theatre of our lives there is ultimately only one member of the audience who matters and that's our Father in heaven.

The Pharisees *"practiced their righteousness before men to be noticed by them"* (Matthew 6:1). The audience they played to were people of social importance. It was their ovations they craved. Their charity work was done to be seen and applauded by others (6:2). Likewise, their prayers were performed in public to garner the praise of others (6:5).

Jesus makes it clear that those who live their life playing to the audience of prominent people, or for public opinion, receive no heavenly applause or reward from our Father in heaven (6:1). However, he also tells us that those interested in pleasing only the Father can fully expect applause from above – and heavenly garlands, tributes and crowns, in this life and the life to come.

I recall a close friend of the family coming down from Scotland to stay at our house. She brought her daughter with her, who was around nine at the time. Her father is a well-known entertainer and her mother a successful dancer, turned dance teacher. Sweetly, her daughter decided to put on a show just for me. I thought it would just be a quick song or a little dance, but she spent the whole day preparing for it. When the performance took place I was deeply moved by the both the time and effort she had spent in creating, producing and starring in a show, just for me! Years later she is now on her way to a successful career performing in Starlight Express, but I will always remember the tremendous honour of being her audience of one.

If I felt special as an audience of one, how do you think the Father feels when we speak and act, conscious above all else, that we are in his presence? We are under his gaze all of the time. Let us then act appropriately in thought, word and deed.

On another occasion I had to meet with someone in a disciplinary scenario. This person had been really out of order in their actions towards others. Have you ever met a really nasty Christian? Of course you have – and this was one of them! I was ready to be the judge, jury and executioner; their time of reckoning had arrived. But I had recently been meditating on the audience of one and I thought to myself, "How would I conduct this meeting if Jesus was physically here, in this room, witnessing the entire meeting?" That thought made me change my attitude.

Just before the meeting, instead of arranging two chairs, I put out three: one for me, one for the other person, and one for the Lord. I decided that I would consciously conduct the meeting as if God was sitting in the empty chair, appraising me as I handled the situation. Although it was still a difficult meeting, it turned out a lot better than it otherwise would have, simply because I was conscious of pleasing my audience of one. Because I desired only to please the Father, it made a big difference to my attitude and conduct, and indeed to the other person's response.

A Royal command performance

If life is a stage, then we all know by now that human audiences are a fickle lot. One day people adored Jesus, the next day they wanted to crucify him. We will never please people, so it's better that we focus on the one who matters.

Your life is like a royal command performance, laid on especially for your Heavenly Father who is sitting in the royal box, while the Holy Spirit prompts you from the wings. Heaven's spotlight is constantly on you and you are always centre stage in the Father's eyes. Perform for his pleasure, and his alone.

Stick to the script

God's script for your life has already been written, spanning the day you were born to the day you die. Each morning you wake up you enter a new scene of your life story. Some seem very mundane, like getting the children ready for school and doing chores. Others are full of life-changing excitement, like a successful job interview or moving into a new house in a new town. But each story scene is part of God's overall plan. The mundane parts are preparing you to handle the more exciting ones.

Whatever part of the story you are currently in, know that not one bit of God's screenplay for your life is wasted. But how do we make sure we are following God's script and not going off course?

Can you imagine an actor arrogantly altering the script of *As You Like It* because they feel they know what works better than Shakespeare? Similarly, we need to follow Father God's script for our life, as laid out in the Bible. Through Scripture we learn how Jesus acts and speaks, so that we can copy his example. Then, we allow the Holy Spirit to guide and direct us. When we start making up our own production script and doing what we like, that's when things start to go seriously wrong.

I'm not talking about making mistakes. None of us are perfect and following the Lord is a lifelong learning experience. In his grace, the Father even allows for our imperfections in his script for our life. But as far as we are able, by his grace and the power of the Holy Spirit, we should endeavour to stick to the script of what the Bible teaches us about how to live our Christian lives.

Your secret legacy

"And your Father who sees in secret will reward you." (Matthew 6:4)

Prominent people in society often come to the place later in life where they are chiefly concerned with what legacy they will leave. What will they leave behind once they are gone? How will people remember them? Winston Churchill once said, "History will be kind to me, for I intend to write it!"

Newspapers publish the obituaries of the famous. In fact, most have a file of obituaries already written for famous people, in case they die suddenly! Typically, these statements celebrate their accomplishments in life and offer a few personal anecdotes.

Guess what? God the Father has also been preparing his obituary for each person's life. While newspaper obituaries offer a record of a person's known public/personal life, the Lord's record includes the unknown, hidden lives of every person who ever lived. His opinions are perfectly accurate because he also takes into account the hidden motives of the heart, not just external words and deeds.

This year the evangelist Billy Graham went to be with the Lord. Before he died, someone asked him what he'd like people to say about him when he'd gone. He replied,

"I want to hear one person say something nice about me and that's the Lord. When I face him I want him to say to me, 'Well done thou good and faithful servant.'"

Pleasing the Father takes great faith and trust, because often no one will know the hidden sacrifice, secret restraint, private anguish in prayer that you have suffered behind the scenes. But your audience of one sees it all.

Why, if you live only for an audience of one and his reward, you will soon be able even to begin loving your enemies!

Love your enemies?

Jesus taught,

> "You have heard that it was said, 'You shall love your neighbour and hate your enemy.' But I say to you, love your enemies and pray for those who persecute you, so that you may be sons of your Father who is in heaven. For he makes his sun rise on the evil and on the good, and sends rain on the just and on the unjust. For if you love those who love you, what reward do you have? Do not even the tax collectors do the same? And if you greet only your brothers, what more are you doing than others? Do not

even the Gentiles do the same? You therefore must be perfect, as your heavenly Father is perfect." (Matthew 5:43-48)

At first glance, the principles and character traits Jesus teaches in the Sermon on the Mount can seem impractical, self-destructive even. Turning the other cheek, going a second mile having being forced to do the first, offering a coat to a person currently suing you for a shirt, giving and lending to whoever asks…

And then the hardest of all: loving your enemies!

Your enemy has no real power over you

We can only love our enemies when we truly understand that they have no real power over us. Why? Because our Father in heaven is in control of our destiny. Believing that Father God is totally in control of everything and everyone (including our enemies), all of the time, requires growing levels of trust.

Jesus believed this about his Father. He understood that no one could harm him until his hour had come, and then it would only be by the Father's permission. Because of this, he could love all people – even those who were committed to crucifying him. They were unwittingly cooperating with the Father's plan, even though they thought they were successfully opposing it (Acts 2:23).

Remember Joseph's brothers who sold him into slavery? They meant to harm him, but through their actions God meant to bless him. Joseph eventually understood this, which made it so much easier for him to forgive them:

"As for you, you meant evil against me, but God meant it for good, to bring it about that many people should be kept alive, as they are today." (Genesis 50:20)

Having an unshakeable faith in God's goodness, even when people are doing evil against you – that is hard-core Spirit-filled living! Knowing that your life is in God's hands, not your enemies', enables you to transcend their evil acts and love them.

When you feel angry or bitter towards someone, it's usually because you sense they are blocking and frustrating your goals. Maybe you feel they are misrepresenting your motives and tampering with your destiny? You fear that they may try to dominate you and hurt you. Feelings like this make us want to fight back, to defeat our adversaries. However, what we really need to do is take this serious situation to the Lord in prayer. Talk to him about it as many times as necessary, until you have confidence that God is in control and that his will is going to be done. You can love your enemies when you know you are not ultimately under their control. This confidence comes through believing prayer.

There is so much more regarding Spirit filled living to be discovered in the Sermon on the Mount, but even if you just implement the little shared in this chapter, you will find yourself advancing in the kingdom of God by leaps and bounds.

If you begin to earnestly apply the teaching of Jesus' sermon to your daily life, with the Spirit's help you will soon look on the outside very much like the Isaac you are on the inside.

CHAPTER 8
YOU SHALL
RECEIVE POWER

"But ye shall receive power, after that the Holy Ghost is come upon you: and ye shall be witnesses unto me both in Jerusalem, and in all Judaea, and in Samaria, and unto the uttermost part of the earth."

(Acts 1:8 KJV)

In Scripture, being filled with the Holy Spirit is connected to spiritual power. What does it mean to receive "power" from the Holy Spirit? And what is power in the first place? The best definition I know comes in the form of an equation:

Power = Motive + Resources

When God blesses us, he also empowers us. Perhaps that's why he takes time to prepare us for receiving more of the Holy Spirit. He knows that his resources can so easily be squandered and abused through self-interest.

The early church received power for a purpose. The Holy Ghost's motive in giving us his resources is the same now as it was then: to enable us to spread the gospel of Jesus far and wide.

The Magus motive

In Acts we read about a man called Simon Magus. He boasted about his great magical power and the people even called him, *"The Great Power of God"* (Acts 8:10). Yet when Magus saw the evangelist Philip, empowered by the Holy Ghost performing signs and miracles, he was flabbergasted. Magus then observed the apostles Peter and John praying for Samaritans who received the Holy Spirit mightily. Magus offered them money in return for allowing him to wield similar power. He wanted the resources of the Holy Spirit, but his motives were completely wrong. Philip, Peter and John were motivated to win souls for Christ and the Holy Spirit resourced them to do so, generating divine gospel power! Magus' motive was entirely selfish.

> *"But Peter said to him, 'May your silver perish with you, because you thought you could obtain the gift of God with money! You have neither part nor lot in this matter, for your heart is not right before God.'"* (Acts 8:20-21)

Simon Magus wasn't ready for more of the Holy Spirit because he didn't want God's power to bless others – he wanted it to make himself great. Peter warned him that with such an attitude he, and his money, would surely perish. As Martyn Lloyd-Jones once said, "The worst thing that can happen to a man is to succeed before he is ready."

Many people have become ruined by their own success, because they didn't attend to the motivation of their hearts. Without a heart that is right before God, seeds of pride, selfishness and greed are planted that sooner or later sprout up and produce a harvest of shame and devastation, damaging others along the way.

Blessed to be a blessing

"And I will make of you a great nation, and I will bless you and make your name great, so that you will be a blessing." (Genesis 12:2)

God gives us the resources of the Holy Spirit expecting that our motivation will be to love and serve others. Abraham was blessed in order to be a blessing. He and his descendants were going to become so great so that they would have enormous spiritual resources to benefit others who had none.

The gospel is the power of God, saving all who believe, and the reason the Holy Spirit is working so deeply in our hearts is to make us whole, so that he can use us to reach out to others with God's saving, healing love. Love activates the Holy Spirit's resources, generating divine power to bless and deliver other people.

"A new commandment I give to you, that you love one another: just as I have loved you, you also are to love one another." (John 13:34)

Jesus instructed us,

"All authority in heaven and on earth has been given to me. Go therefore and make disciples of all nations, baptizing them in the name of the Father and of the Son and of the Holy Spirit." (Matthew 28:18-19)

In our quest to imitate the character of Isaac, let's make sure that we become a Philip and not a Magus.

Chapter 9
The Fruit of the Holy Spirit

"But the fruit of the Spirit is love, joy, peace, patience, kindness, goodness, faithfulness, gentleness, self-control; against such things there is no law."

(Galatians 5: 22-23)

How many books have been written about the gifts of the Spirit, miracles, prophecy and the like? Too many to count. How many books have been written about the fruit of the Spirit? Too few to mention.

Many of us can name the nine gifts of the Spirit without blinking, but struggle to recall the nine fruit of the Spirit. Yet, if the major work of the Holy Spirit is cultivation of his fruit within our hearts, how can we cooperate with his activity if we don't know what this fruit is?

The two Pentecosts

It was no coincidence that the Holy Spirit was poured out on the Day of Pentecost. The first Pentecost brought the Law of Moses, but the Acts 2 Pentecost brought the Holy Spirit. The Mosaic Law can't save us, nor can it sanctify us. The Holy Spirit was given on the day of Pentecost to replace the Law, making it now redundant in the life of the Christian. Old Testament legal codes, commands and moral regulations were entirely replaced by the Person and work of the Holy Spirit.

> *"But if you are led by the Spirit, you are not under the law."* (Galatians 5:18)

Paul speaks about the life of the Spirit and the works of "flesh". The works of the flesh are evident in people who try to make life work without God (Galatians 5:19). Paul rightly calls them "works" because living according to fleshly strategies is exhausting. Trying to get through life depending on our self-effort exacts a terrible price from those who try it. Remember Jacob?

But the Holy Spirit produces fruit in our lives. Fruit is defined as a seed-bearing structure that develops from a flowering plant. The fruit produced bears the nature of its parent plant. Healthy apple trees produce apples; heathy orange trees bear oranges.

When you were "born again" God gave you a new nature (2 Corinthians 5:17) because the old you was like a bad tree that could only produce bad fruit. The new you is like a brand new tree that if properly cultivated can produce all the fruit of the Holy Spirit! Being a Christian is all about walking out of the shadow of your old sinful life and allowing the "new you" to bear the fruit of the Spirit for everyone around to enjoy.

Love, all the time

A celebrated Christian theologian was at death's door. Lying on his death bed, weak and fading fast his family sat by. Suddenly, his countenance changed and his face lit up with a beaming smile. He lifted his hands to heaven and exclaimed with joy:

"I see it, I see it! Now I understand. It was love, love all the time."

After saying this he bowed his head and passed away.

A touching story perhaps, but there is a lesson to be learnt here. This great, gifted Bible teacher only understood the supremacy of love moments before dying. We need to grasp this truth and live by it today. If we are to live out of our Isaac identities, then we are to be known as people of love.

As Paul pointed out,

> *"For the whole law is fulfilled in one word: 'You shall love your neighbour as yourself.'"* (Galatians 5:14)

He was reiterating the teaching of Jesus. Christ commanded us to love one another and taught that the sum total of the Christian life is found in one word: love.

But what is love? Is it an emotional feeling? Attraction? An attitude of lenient tolerance towards the faults of others? The apostle John defines love for us in the Person of the Father:

> *"In this is love, not that we have loved God but that he loved us and sent his Son to be the propitiation for our sins."* (1 John 4:10)

God's love does not excuse or avoid the issue of human sin, but rather challenges it head on. The word "propitiation" is avoided by some translators, who find it too unpalatable a term to be used – despite it being the actual word in the Greek text.

"Propitiation" means the act of appeasing an angry God. God is both rightly and appropriately angry about our human sin. Nonetheless, the good news is that in his love for us, God punished his son in our place, satisfying his justice while also displaying his love. All we have to do is believe this and we are saved from his wrath forever. Once saved from our sins, we are ready to experience his wonderful love, poured out in our hearts through the Holy Spirit.

If John defines what God's love is, then how should we respond? When Jesus commanded us to love one another what did he envision that love looking like?

> *"But the fruit of the Spirit is love, joy, peace, patience, kindness, goodness, faithfulness, gentleness, self-control; against such things there is no law."* (Galatians 5:22)

In the above verse we read about the fruit (singular) of the Spirit, not the fruits (plural). The fruit of the Spirit is love – the other eight words simply describe what Christian love looks like.

Love divine, all loves excelling

Christian love is supernaturally produced. Only the Holy Spirit can produce the fruit of divine love in our hearts. We can't do it without him. The eight words describing what love looks like are also spiritual qualities that proceed only from the Holy Spirit. I have heard some people say that they were patient, kind or self-controlled before they became Christians, as if these fruits could be cultivated without the help of the Holy Spirit. This is nonsense.

The fruit of the Spirit are as supernatural as the gifts of the Spirit. If you ever meet a Christian who is highly developed in the fruit of the Spirit, you will be amazed by how they speak and act. It's like witnessing a living miracle because that person has indeed become a supernatural work of God, fashioned by the Spirit.

These eight words used to describe this supernatural love are far more powerful in the original Greek language than in their English translations. Here is a sense of what they actually mean:

- **Love** is the "God kind" of love which excels all other types of love. It is described by the below eight qualities:

- **Joy** – the emotional feeling that comes from fresh encounters with the Holy Spirit and the truth of God's Word.

- **Peace** – the wholeness, assurance, confidence, security and prosperity of soul that comes only from trusting in the Lord alone.

- **Patience** – better translated "long-tempered". The word really means a gritty, determined resolve that never gives up.

- **Kindness** – reflects an attitude that remains positive towards people, even when they don't deserve it.

- **Goodness** – a big-hearted generosity to others, both in word and deed.

- **Faith or faithfulness** – reflects a profound trust in God with a subsequent faithfulness to his will.

- **Gentleness** – strength, authority and power kept under control for the benefit of others.

- **Self-control** – yielding to the Holy Spirit and allowing him to take a "powerful grip" upon your whole life

In my book on Galatians, *No more Law!* (Paternoster, 2012) I give a fuller study of these nine fruit of the Spirit, helping you see what love might look like in any given situation.

Pause for a moment and consider your present circumstances. Which of the above fruit is God developing in your life today? Can you identify them? Perhaps you now know how you could better cooperate with the Holy Spirit this week.

Love is…

The fruit of the Spirit is so powerful, however, that it cannot adequately be expressed in nine words. That's why Christian love is described in many other chapters in the Bible, such as the famous "Love is" chapter, 1 Corinthians 13. Like Paul, James also refers to the fruit of the Spirit, but uses a different term, calling it the "wisdom from above":

> *"But the wisdom from above is first pure, then peaceable, gentle, open to reason, full of mercy and good fruits, impartial and sincere. And a harvest of righteousness is sown in peace by those who make peace."* (James 3:17-18)

The Beatitudes of Matthew 5 we've already discussed is yet another way of speaking about the fruit of the Spirit. Indeed, wherever we find Christian virtues listed in the New Testament we are reading a description of the fruit of the Spirit (e.g., Philippians 2:1-15; Colossians 3:12-17; 1 Thessalonians 5:12-21).

Your spiritual appraisal

Have you ever had a review at work? Usually your line manager will give a comprehensive evaluation of your performance, highlighting your strengths and identifying weaknesses to work on in the coming year. Imagine if, today, God invited you to a spiritual appraisal!

Where would the Lord start with your spiritual appraisal? What would be his top priority for discussion? Would he start with the strength of your prayer life? Or perhaps your daily Bible reading and study of Scripture? Would he examine your church service and small group attendance patterns? Or would he print out a copy of your financial giving to the church and charities?

All these are important issues, but I believe that the issue at the top of the Father's agenda would be, "How are you treating other people?" John writes,

> *"We love because he first loved us. If anyone says, 'I love God,' and hates his brother, he is a liar; for he who does not love his brother whom he has seen cannot love God whom he has not seen. And this commandment we have from him: whoever loves God must also love his brother."* (1 John 4:19-21)

As the Holy Spirit works in our lives, his greatest desire is to see a rich harvest of his fruit of love. Love that reaches out to a lost and dying world filled with selfish unloveliness.

When the Holy Spirit comes in power, and God blesses you to become a blessing, none of it will mean anything without love. So then, in all you are pursuing in life, make sure you pursue love.

> *"If I speak in the tongues of men and of angels, but have not love, I am a noisy gong or a clanging cymbal. And if I have prophetic powers, and understand all mysteries and all knowledge, and if I have all faith, so as to remove mountains, but have not love, I am nothing. If I give away all I have, and if I deliver up my body to be burned, but have not love, I gain nothing.*

Love is patient and kind; love does not envy or boast; it is not arrogant or rude. It does not insist on its own way; it is not irritable or resentful; it does not rejoice at wrongdoing, but rejoices with the truth. Love bears all things, believes all things, hopes all things, endures all things.

Love never ends. As for prophecies, they will pass away; as for tongues, they will cease; as for knowledge, it will pass away. For we know in part and we prophesy in part, but when the perfect comes, the partial will pass away. When I was a child, I spoke like a child, I thought like a child, I reasoned like a child. When I became a man, I gave up childish ways. For now we see in a mirror dimly, but then face to face. Now I know in part; then I shall know fully, even as I have been fully known.

So now faith, hope, and love abide, these three; but the greatest of these is love."

(1 Corinthians 13)

Chapter 10
His Spirit Answers to the Blood

"And to Jesus, the mediator of a new covenant, and to the sprinkled blood that speaks a better word than the blood of Abel."

(Hebrews 12:24)

"You'll be preaching and pleading the blood each week then?" said my friend Mark when he heard I was going to Bible school at Kensington Temple (a Pentecostal church in the heart of Notting Hill Gate, London). I looked at him with a puzzled expression. I had no idea what he was talking about. "You'll find out," he said and we left it at that.

I later discovered that most modern day Pentecostals now frown upon the practice of what is known as "pleading the blood".

This practice was prevalent in earlier pioneer days of the Pentecostal movement. Whatever pleading the blood was in those early days, as time passed it became something of a superstitious repeated mantra, spoken over people and circumstances to ensure spiritual protection. Some thought that if you hadn't spoken the protection of the blood of Jesus over a situation or person they would somehow be left open and exposed to the devil's power.

Despite hearing about the abuses of "pleading the blood", something inside told me that there was more to it than I had been told. During research for my book on the history of revivals in Great Britain, I discovered that sometimes unique Holy Spirit emphases in particular revivals had later developed into human superstition or tradition (*Land of Hope and Glory*, Dovewell Publications, 2003).

The Gospel of Blood

The church today is in grave danger of devaluing the most precious commodity in the universe – the blood of Jesus – which purchased salvation for all who believe.

> *"Be on guard for yourselves and for all the flock, among which the Holy Spirit has made you overseers, to shepherd **the church of God which He purchased with His own blood**."* (Acts 20:28 NASB)

Our gospel is primarily a gospel of blood. Most Westerners don't like to think about blood. It's commonly viewed as icky and sticky! We live in western societies where we don't have to personally kill chickens, lambs or cows for our meat. I think if I had to wring a chicken's neck for dinner time I would turn vegetarian straightaway. Even if I pick up a packet of bacon rashers at the supermarket and see a tiny spot of blood, I'll put it back and choose another one that's clean!

I believe this cultural aversion to blood has permeated our theology too. We are content to speak about Christ's death on the cross, but we hardly mention his blood – yet Scripture is full of it. The Bible loves to speak about the blood of Jesus! In the New Testament the blood of Christ is mentioned five times more than the death of Christ and three times more than the cross.

The blood speaks

The Bible teaches us that sacrificial blood actually speaks to God. We read in Genesis that the blood of Abel literally cried out for justice to the Lord and he heard.

> "And the LORD said, 'What have you done? The voice of your brother's blood is crying to me from the ground.'" (Genesis 4:10)

In the book of Exodus, the Israelites smeared the blood of lambs on their door posts and when God's angel of judgement saw the blood, he passed over that dwelling place and no one died.

In the Jerusalem temple, blood flowed like a river from the altar every day, and when God saw the blood of sacrifice it affected him so powerfully that he responded with mercy rather than judgment.

The New Covenant itself was baptised in the blood of Jesus:

> "For this is my blood of the covenant, which is poured out for many for the forgiveness of sins." (Matthew 26:28)

Before the Holy Spirit could be poured out on the Day of Pentecost, Jesus had to ascend into heaven for a very special occasion. Entering into heaven's eternal Holy of Holies, the Son presented his Father with the very blood he had shed on the cross for the sins of the world. This must have been a tremendously emotionally charged moment for the Father, to be formally presented with the sacrificial blood of his own dear Son. The blood spoke mercy and the Father's response was to send the gift of the Holy Spirit to the church. It was the most merciful thing he could have done in response to being presented with the blood.

The Spirit answers to the blood

Like our Father in heaven, I too have an only son. His name is Jake, but I wouldn't give his life for any of you (sorry!) If he died and you brought me the evidence of his death, a blood soaked jacket perhaps, the sight of it would be both devastating and overpowering. Whenever someone applies the blood of Jesus to their life by believing in his death and resurrection, the Spirit sees the blood over their lives and it is so attractive to him that he comes to dwell in them forever. The eternal blood of Jesus has the most incredibly profound effect on both the Father and the Holy Spirit.

One of Charles Wesley's most beautiful hymns is *Arise, My Soul, Arise*. It is permeated with powerful truths about the blood of Jesus. Note in the third verse that there is an often-quoted phrase which is a key to understanding the relationship between the blood and the Spirit: *His Spirit answers to the blood.*

Arise, my soul, arise; shake off thy guilty fears;
The bleeding Sacrifice in my behalf appears:
Before the throne my surety stands,
My name is written on His hands.
He ever lives above, for me to intercede;
His all-redeeming love, His precious blood to plead:
His blood atoned for all our race,
And sprinkles now the throne of grace.

Five bleeding wounds He bears, received on Calvary;
They pour effectual prayers; they strongly plead for me:
"Forgive him, oh, forgive," they cry,
"Nor let that ransomed sinner die!"

The Father hears Him pray, His dear anointed One;
He cannot turn away the presence of His Son;
His Spirit answers to the blood,
And tells me I am born of God.

You're a Priest!

Whatever God calls you to be in your career, community or local congregation, your primary calling from the Lord is to be his priest.

> *"But you are a chosen race, a royal priesthood, a holy nation, a people for his own possession, that you may proclaim the excellencies of him who called you out of darkness into his marvellous light."* (1 Peter 2:9)

What is the role of a priest? Essentially, a true priest represents the people before God and also God before the people. All

Christians are priests. There is no such thing as a specially ordained priesthood within the church. Any divide between laity and clergy is a man-made construct and biblically absurd. All of us are ordained priests the moment that we believe in Jesus.

Because our primary calling in this life is to be priests, we need to intercede for one another and for a lost and dying world; mediate and stand in the gap through prayer and proclamation. Think about this: in your neighbourhood, workplace or school you may be the only priest of the living God anyone has contact with. Perhaps you are the only one who is in a position to speak their names before the throne of God's mercy in prayer and witness to them about the love of God?

Priests plead the blood

Earlier I mentioned I had a feeling there was more to the "pleading of the blood" than I'd been told by my Pentecostal colleagues. Over the years I have dug deep into Classical Pentecostal heritage. I discovered that in the early years of the Pentecostal outpouring in Great Britain (early 1900s) there was a powerful prophetic movement that stressed the importance of the blood of Jesus.

Even people such as the relatively famous Anglican minister Alexander Boddy, who was used in the wonderful Sunderland outpouring, were powerfully influenced by this movement. Here is an account about Boddy attending a meeting which emphasised the importance of Christ's sacrificial blood, from Kent White's book The Word of God Coming Again (Apostolic Faith Church, Winton, Bournemouth, 1919):

> "Rev. A.A Boddy of Sunderland came and saw them pleading the Blood, falling under the power and speaking in tongues.

He was so overcome he lay on the platform on his face, unable to speak. He told pastor Murdoch that he had been in Norway, in Barret's meetings, and that the power of the Holy Ghost was more manifest in Kilsyth than it was there; in fact, than in any place he had ever been. Then he and Mrs Boddy pled the Blood in their meetings in Sunderland. In Sunderland the baptisms they had had at first, without pleading the Blood, had practically ceased, and John Martin was sent down there, and commenced pleading the Blood; the power of the Spirit was manifest anew, and many were baptised … When the Blood pleading commenced, there was no preaching, exhortation, or remarks on the subject; it came spontaneously under the strong expulsive power of the Holy Ghost."

This strong emphasis on the blood of Jesus resulted in a spontaneous outpouring of the Holy Spirit. It wasn't done in a legalistic or superstitious way (not yet anyway). God was somehow emphasising the honouring of the blood.

I have often pondered that if we are the "priesthood of all believers", as we boldly approach the throne of God's grace in priestly intercession, do we give thought to the truth that all biblical priestly ministry is established on sacrificial blood? When we pray, we are able to approach God only through the blood of Jesus shed at Calvary.

I've also been meditating about how Christ's blood must still have an irresistible effect on the Father. Without that blood, why should God answer any of our prayers? Without the blood, on what basis should we expect that he may once again grant a Holy Spirit revival to a backslidden Europe? Is it possible to persuade the Father to send us more of his Holy Spirit? What would persuade him to do this? Surely by appealing to the powerful blood of Christ's sacrifice?

> *"Knowing that you were ransomed from the futile ways inherited from your forefathers, not with perishable things such as silver or gold, but with the precious blood of Christ, like that of a lamb without blemish or spot."* (1 Peter 1:18-19)

I don't think we value the blood of Jesus enough today. Peter believes Christ's blood is even more precious than gold or silver. The blood of Jesus is the most valuable thing in the whole universe. It paid off the debt of human sin! Do we really appreciate or honour it enough? Without an awareness and gratefulness for Christ's sacrificial blood we will always have a tendency to self-righteousness. We expect God to answer our prayers, but why should he? We think he should vindicate us, bless us, favour us and deliver us, but on what basis are we so confident? I am gradually realising how frail, weak and sinful I am in myself. I am coming to the conclusion that there is only one reason that God would do anything for me, and that's because Jesus' blood was shed on my behalf.

That's my only plea before his throne. I don't have any other reason to expect him to respond. He loved me so much he shed his blood for me. Yet in weakness I have a growing confidence in the power of the blood shed on my behalf. It speaks mercy and grace about me. It hides me and covers me from judgement. The blood speaks better things for me and I keep asking the Father to be merciful to me because of the blood of his Son. He can't resist the blood of his Son and I know he will come to my aid because of it. It's my only plea for help – but it's the only plea I need!

Pleading the blood is not a ritualistic, repetitive mouthing of a slogan. Rather it is approaching the Father with a bold awareness that Christ's shed blood is our greatest plea before him. Might I even say that the blood of Jesus is an irresistible plea for God to be merciful and answer our prayers? We'd have no right to pray in the "name of Jesus" if there hadn't been shed blood to give us the right to do so.

God loves to be reminded of his covenant. That is why the Lord's Supper is so important. When we remind him of the blood it spurs him to redemptive action. The blood is the evidence that Christ died. The blood gives God the reason to act in mercy, and the most merciful thing he can do for us is to send more of his Spirit. More Lord!

A friend of mine once prayed the following declaration:

A plea to the Father

Our Father in heaven,

We can't think of any reason for you to answer our prayers except that your Son shed his blood for us. We have no other plea before your throne of grace, except that the blood of Jesus speaks of better things than we are experiencing right now. Avert your gaze from our self-righteousness and instead see us through the blood-tinted lens of Calvary. As priestly intercessors we plead the Saviour's blood before you. The blood is our sole confidence in requesting that you would graciously send us more of your Holy Spirit.

Holy Spirit, we ask that you would increase your powerful presence among us because Jesus shed his blood for you to come and live in our lives. Please answer the blood sacrifice of Jesus by coming to us with more of the fire of your presence and power.

Amen.

If that type of prayer is "pleading the blood", then my friend Mark was indeed a prophet that day.

CHAPTER 11
WHAT TO EXPECT DURING A REVIVAL

"And when he came up out of the water, immediately he saw the heavens being torn open and the Spirit descending on him like a dove. And a voice came from heaven, 'You are my beloved Son; with you I am well pleased.' The Spirit immediately drove him out into the wilderness. And he was in the wilderness forty days, being tested by Satan. And he was with the wild animals, and the angels were ministering to him."

(Mark 1:10-13)

"Then he said to the man, 'Stretch out your hand.' And the man stretched it out, and it was restored, healthy like the other. But the Pharisees went out and conspired against him, how to destroy him." (Matthew 12:13-14)

For the first thirty years of Jesus' life he lived in obscurity. He performed no miracles, cast out no demons and none of the religious leaders even knew his name. All that dramatically changed from the moment he was baptised in the Holy Spirit. At that moment began a three year revival of the works of God in Israel.

The Holy Spirit is always at work in the church, but sometimes quietly. During these quiet periods people still get saved, but not that many. The gifts of the Spirit are manifested but not too often. Demonic powers are broken but many still remain enthroned. When the Holy Spirt comes in revival power it isn't that his "job description" changes – he still does exactly what he was doing in the quieter times – the difference is that in revival he works with a far greater intensity, power and demonstration.

When the Holy Spirit moves in revival power, many surprising and unexpected things can occur, but you can be sure that in such outpourings three features will always be evident:

1. The works of the Spirit.

2. Fleshly reactions

3. Demonic manifestations

1. The works of the Spirit

"A revival, then, really means days of heaven upon earth." – Martyn Lloyd-Jones

Although I am highlighting three features of revival, the works of the Spirit are most prominent of the three. Having been baptised in the Holy Spirit, Jesus then ministered three years with an unlimited measure of the Spirit's anointing and empowering (John 3:34). The gospels record the incredible miracles, healings and salvations that took place under our Lord's ministry. When the Holy Spirit comes to us in seasons of great revival power, be ready for an incredible harvest of souls, powerful holiness encounters, incredible manifestations of the gifts of the Holy Spirit and great experiences of God's tangible presence and glory.

2. Fleshly reactions

We would all expect an intensifying of the works of the Spirit during a revival, but how many of us would expect an outbreak of fleshly behaviour in response? But the works of the flesh are evident (Galatians 5:19-21) and are all rooted in unbelief and selfishness. The Holy Spirit hates the flesh and the flesh hates the Holy Spirit (Galatians 5:16-17). The Pharisees were so jealous of the Holy Spirit's ministry through Jesus that they conspired to destroy him. Jesus brought out the worst in them. In seasons of revival, the Holy Spirit unearths, provokes and brings to the light undercurrents of fleshly jealousy, unbelief, pride and greed. The Holy Spirit incites the flesh in our lives, fully intending to deliver us from it – but only if we are willing.

In seasons of great outpourings of the Holy Spirit, don't panic if at times you feel like the most rotten Christian in the world. God is just revealing the impurities in your heart so that he can heal you from them. If you soften your heart, healing joy will replace your godly sorrow very quickly.

The Pharisees, however, were not willing to be delivered from their carnality. They didn't even think they were fleshly; they believed that they were the godly ones! To them the Holy Spirit was the bad guy; they thought his works were demonic. So their carnality gradually worsened during the powerful Holy Spirit visitation. For the unyielding Pharisees it would have been better for them if revival had never come, because they just hardened their hearts, ready to reap an even greater judgment than they were under before.

3. Demonic manifestation

The first thing the Holy Spirit did after Jesus was baptised in the river Jordan was to "throw" or "drive" him out into the wilderness for a confrontation with the devil. It was the Holy Spirit's top priority! For the rest of his ministry, Jesus didn't need to seek out demonic power. He could hardly walk down a high street without them manifesting and crying out! Demonic powers will operate reasonably quietly when they are left to reign in society, relatively unchallenged. But just as the Holy Ghost incites the flesh to conquer it, so he provokes and disturbs demonic powers with a view to casting them down.

Some have dismissed past revivals as "not of God" because they witnessed human fleshliness or demonic manifestations. But let's be realistic, in revival outpourings we should expect to see powerful workings of the Spirit and his provoking of both the flesh and demonic powers. When the Spirit comes in power in your life, he will do wonderful, joyful, amazing things in and through you. He will also, at times, allow your fleshly desires to be provoked and any demonic strongholds to be revealed. When this happens, although uncomfortable for you at the time, know that he is doing this to liberate you from such oppressions and bring you into new levels of glorious gospel freedom.

Chapter 12
It's time to seek the Lord

"Sow righteousness for yourselves, reap unfailing love. Break up the unplowed ground for yourselves, for it is time to seek the Lord, until he comes and showers deliverance on you."

(Hosea 10:12 NET Bible)

Hosea 10:12 was the text of the first sermon I ever preached. It tells us that now is the time to seek the Lord. Today!

As I said at the beginning of this book, seeking the Lord is an end in itself. The process of prayer can also be an end in itself. As can the pursuit of revival. Why? Because in the act of seeking, asking and pursuing God, some of the greatest works of the Holy Spirit are being accomplished in our lives.

The journey counts even more than the destination.

> *"And so I tell you, keep on asking, and you will receive what you ask for. Keep on seeking, and you will find. Keep on knocking, and the door will be opened to you."* (Luke 11:9 NLT)

Today we have instant everything. We want something and we expect to get it, NOW! But that is not the way God works. Jesus spent thirty years in preparation for the anointing of the Spirit for a three-year ministry.

Imagine if Abraham had been instantly teleported to the Promised Land during his first meeting with the Lord and a week later Isaac was miraculously born. Imagine if the young lad Joseph had been instantly promoted to Prime Minister of Egypt the day after receiving his special coat. Or the shepherd boy David crowned king hours after being anointed with oil by the prophet Samuel.

There are numerous other examples. What all these biblical characters have in common is that they all waited on God, sought him, and learned to trust him patiently in both good and bad times. The journey of preparation was as valuable as the moment when they received the promised blessing of God. If they had received the blessing instantaneously, what would that have taught them? How would it have matured their faith? They would have missed many opportunities to learn more about God and themselves. They wouldn't have been as grateful as they were, having patiently endured. Maybe too, they simply wouldn't have been ready to handle the blessing when it came.

Having spoken about waiting and seeking, however, I do have a sense that in these days God is quickening his work in our hearts. He is speeding up the process of spiritual maturation. Looking at many young Christians today, I am encouraged to see an accelerated process of Holy Spirit maturing in their lives – far speedier than it happened in my Christian life.

If you learn the lessons of the Holy Spirit quickly and with keenness, you won't need to wander in the wilderness for forty years, you will enter the Promised Land in weeks!

Finally, for all those who still find themselves acting like Jacobs: it's never too late to start making the Isaac factor count in your lives. Nothing is ever wasted with God. He can make up the years that the locust devoured and do it very quickly. I believe that what has happened in the past has been but a preparation for what the Holy Spirit is going to do now in our lives.

William Shakespeare was right when he wrote in The Tempest that, "What's past is prologue."

Come Holy Spirit!

As the Holy Spirit works in our lives, his greatest desire is to see a rich harvest of his fruit of love. Love that reaches out to a lost and dying world filled with selfish unloveliness.

When the Holy Spirit falls comes in power, and God blesses you to become a blessing, none of it will mean anything without love. So then, in all you are pursuing in life, make sure you pursue love.